morning and night prayer

St. Mary's High School

07/04

ST. MARY'S HIGH SCHOOL

Celtic Benediction

Celtic Benediction

Morning and Night Prayer

J PHILIP NEWELL

NOVALIS

To my eldest son
Brendan William Douglas
and to the Artist in him

Illustrations from the Lindisfarne Gospels by
permission of the British Library

Originally published in 2000 in the U.K. by The Canterbury Press

Published in Canada by Novalis. Business office:
49 Front Street East, 2nd Floor, Toronto, Ontario, Canada
M5E 1B3

Canadian Library Catalogue Card No: 00-900505-6

ISBN 2-89507-100-4

Design and Typesetting by Vera Brice
Cover design by Leigh Hurlock

Printed in Singapore by
Tien Wah Press

Contents

Preface

It was during my years on Iona, the little holy island of Scotland in the Western Isles, that I was alerted to the richness of the stream of prayer that flows deep in the Celtic tradition. For centuries prayers chanted at the rising of the sun and its setting, or intoned at the birth of a child or the death of a loved one, had been passed down in the oral tradition from one generation to the next. These prayers of the past spoke to me of a way of seeing that was lost and needed to be recovered again. They communicated a sense of the interweaving of what is seen with what is unseen, of the spiritual world and the world of matter conjoined. There is a yearning among people all over the western world today for a renewed depth of relationship between spirituality and the mystery of creation. Here in our own Christian inheritance is a way of seeing that provides us with models for such a reintegration. I have written the prayers of this book as a new expression of this ancient tradition.

What do we mean by the Celtic tradition? There is such a spectrum of opinion on this matter that some critics have preferred to say that historically no such tradition can be clearly identified. Attention to the writings of early Irish, Welsh and Scottish Christian teachers, however, as well as observation of the poetry, prayers and art of Celtic cultures over the centuries, point to distinctive characteristics of what I believe can be called 'a tradition' of spirituality. There are two major features of the Celtic tradition that distinguish it from what in contrast can be called 'the Mediterranean tradition'. Celtic spirituality is marked by the belief that what is deepest in us is the image of God. Sin has distorted and obscured that image but not erased it. The Mediterranean tradition, on the other hand, in its doctrine of original sin has taught that what is deepest in us is our sinfulness. This has given rise to a tendency to define ourselves in terms of the ugliness of our failings instead of the beauty of our origins. The second major characteristic of the Celtic tradition is a belief in the essential goodness of creation. Not only is creation viewed as a blessing, it is regarded in essence as an expression of God. Thus the great Celtic teachers refer to it as 'the book of creation' in which we may read the mystery of God. The Mediterranean tradition, on the other hand, has tended towards a separation of spirit and matter, and thus has distanced the mystery of God from the matter of creation.

I have explored these two major characteristics in *The Book of Creation: an Introduction to Celtic Spirituality* (1999). The book is based on 'the seven days of creation' from Genesis which are treated as theophanies or 'showings' of God. The light of the first day, for instance, is seen as an expression of the divine light that is at the heart and origin of all life. The second day reflects the wildness of creativity; the third, the earth's fecundity; the fourth, the harmony of masculine and feminine; the fifth, the goodness of the senses; the sixth, the fathomless mystery of humanity made in the image of God; and the seventh, the stillness that is essential to life's renewal. I have allowed these seven expressions of the mystery of God in creation to give shape also to the structure of *Celtic Benediction*. The theme of light, therefore, is woven into the prayers of the first day, as is the uncontainable energy of creativity into the second day, and so on throughout the seven days of the week.

The art used in this book illustrates the spirituality of these prayers. What has come to be referred to as 'the everlasting pattern' in Celtic art, in which one strand is woven together inseparably with another, points to the belief in the interweaving of worlds, of the divine and the human, the angelic and the creaturely, of darkness and light. Never are the spiritual and the physical torn apart. In its depictions of humanity we find interlacing designs patterned into the very flesh of human figures and at the same time the limbs of great creatures entwined around the lower half of the human body. These art forms recognise the creaturely dimensions of who we are without thereby portraying these as essentially bestial, for also woven through our deepest desires and physical energies are the threads of God's light. Redemption in this tradition is about being re-connected to the presence of this glory deep within us and among us in creation.

In each morning and evening prayer I have included a 'Scripture and Meditation' section. There has been no attempt to provide a full cycle of Scripture readings for use throughout the year. A rich selection of lectionaries and other approaches to the daily reading of Scripture is available in our various Christian traditions. What I have attempted to do, in the inclusion of brief sentences from Scripture, is to provide an example of how a simple phrase can be used as the basis for meditation. The oldest forms of meditative prayer in Christian practice consist simply of a repetition of words from Scripture in the silence of the heart. In Celtic spirituality this discipline of silent meditation is viewed as opening the eyes of the heart in order to see God in all things.

There has always been a great love of Scripture in the Celtic stream of spirituality. This is reflected in its most enduring artistic expressions over the centuries. The high-standing crosses include both Scripture imagery and creation imagery. Similarly a passion for Scripture is seen in the magnificent illuminations of psalms and gospel texts in Celtic manuscripts. The Psalms and the Gospels in fact occupy a special place in Celtic artwork and teachings, most notably the Gospel according to St John, whom it is said Jesus 'especially loved'. He was remembered as having leaned against Jesus at the last supper. Celtic legend thereby came to refer to him as the one who had heard the heartbeat of God. He became a symbol of the meditative practice of listening for the Word of Love at the heart of life, the Word that is deeper than any fears and sufferings that we will also hear within us when we listen. My hope is that the Scripture phrases and prayers of this book may draw us further towards such an awareness, and in becoming more aware to become more engaged in acts of love for the life of the world.

J Philip Newell
St Giles' Cathedral
Edinburgh

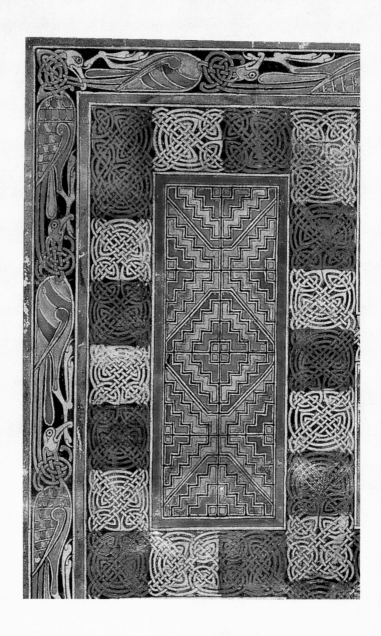

Sunday Morning Prayer

'I wait for you, O God,
my soul waits
and in your word I hope.
My soul waits for you, O God,
more than those who watch for the morning,
more than those who watch for the morning.'

Psalm 130:5-6

SILENCE

*Be still and aware of God's presence within
and all around*

Opening Prayer

I watch this morning
for the light that the darkness has not overcome.
I watch for the fire that was in the beginning
and that burns still in the brilliance of the rising sun.
I watch for the glow of life that gleams in the growing earth
and glistens in sea and sky.
I watch for your light, O God,
in the eyes of every living creature
and in the ever-living flame of my own soul.
If the grace of seeing were mine this day
I would glimpse you in all that lives.
Grant me the grace of seeing this day.
Grant me the grace of seeing.

Scripture and Meditation

'With you is the fountain of life.'

Psalm 36:9

Jesus said, 'I am the light of the world.'

John 8:12

Prayers of Thanksgiving and Intercession

Blessed are you, O Child of the Dawn,
for your light that dapples through creation
on leaves that shimmer in the morning sun
and in showers of rain that wash the earth.
Blessed are you
for the human spirit dappled with eternal light
in its longings for love and birth
and its pain-filled passions and tears.
Blessed are you, O Christ,
for you awaken me to life.
Blessed are you
for you stir me to true desire.

*Pray for the coming day
and for the life of the world*

Closing Prayer

May the light of God
illumine the heart of my soul.
May the flame of Christ
kindle me to love.
May the fire of the Spirit
free me to live
this day, tonight and for ever.

Sunday Night Prayer

'I commune with my heart in the night,
I meditate and search my spirit.'

Psalm 77:6

SILENCE

*Be still and aware of God's presence
within and all around*

Opening Prayer

Out of the silence at the beginning of time
you spoke the Word of life.
Out of the world's primeval darkness
you flooded the universe with light.
In the quiet of this place
in the dark of the night
I wait and watch.
In the stillness of my soul
and from its fathomless depths
the senses of my heart are awake to you.
For fresh soundings of life
for new showings of light
I search in the silence of my spirit, O God.

Scripture and Meditation

'You are my light and my salvation, whom shall I fear?'

Psalm 27:1

'The light shines in the darkness, and the darkness has not overcome it.'

John 1:5

Prayers of Thanksgiving and Intercession

Thanks be to you, O God,
for the night and its light,
for stars that emerge out of evening skies
and the white moon's radiance.
Thanks be to you
for the earth's unfolding of colour
and the bright sheen of creatures from
ocean depths.
In the darknesses of the world
and in the night of my own soul
let me be looking with longing for light
let me be looking in hope.

Recall the events of the day
and pray for the life of the world

Closing Prayer

May the grace of the night's stillness be mine
may the grace of the moon's guidance be mine
may the grace of heaven's vastness be mine
to renew my soul in sleep
to enlighten my dreams in the night
to open my spirit to eternity
until the angels of light awaken me
until the morning angels awaken me.

Monday Morning Prayer

'You are wrapped in light as with a garment, O God,
you ride on the wings of the wind.' *Psalm 104:2-3*

SILENCE

*Be still and aware of God's presence within
and all around*

Opening Prayer

For the morning light
and its irresistible dawning,
for your untameable utterances of life
in boundless stretches of space
and the strength of the waves of the sea
I give you thanks, O God.
Release in me the power of your Spirit
that my soul may be free
and my spirit strong.
Release in me the freedom of your Spirit
that I may be bridled by nothing but love
that I may be bridled only by love.

Scripture and Meditation

'You are my strength, O God, and I love you.'

Psalm 18:1

Jesus said, 'Out of your heart shall flow rivers
of living water.'

John 7:38

Prayers of Thanksgiving and Intercession

For the might of your wind on the waters
for the swelling of the open sea
and the rushing of crested waves
thanks be to you, O God.
For the strength of desire in my body
for the sap of life that flows
and the yearnings for birth and abundance
thanks be to you.
Restore me in the image of your love this day
that the longings of my heart may be true.
Restore me in the image of your love this day
that my passions for life may be full.

Pray for the coming day
and for the life of the world

Closing Prayer

In the beginning, O God,
your Spirit swept over the chaotic deep like a wild wind
and creation was born.
In the turbulence of my own life
and the unsettled waters of the world today
let there be new birthings of your Spirit.
In the currents of my own heart
and the upheavals of the world today
let there be new birthings of your mighty Spirit.

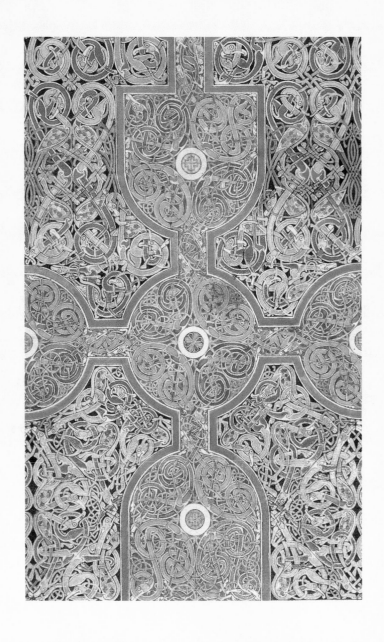

Monday Night Prayer

'Before the mountains were brought forth,
or ever you had formed the earth,
from everlasting to everlasting you are God.'

Psalm 90:2

SILENCE

*Be still and aware of God's presence within
and all around*

Opening Prayer

In the infinity of night skies
in the free flashing of lightning
in whirling elemental winds
you are God.
In the impenetrable mists of dark clouds
in the wild gusts of lashing rain
in the ageless rocks of the sea
you are God and I bless you.
You are in all things
and contained by no thing.
You are the Life of all life
and beyond every name.
You are God and in the eternal mystery I praise you.

Scripture and Meditation

'Happy are those whose strength is in you.'

Psalm 84:5

Jesus said, 'The wind blows where it chooses,
and you hear the sound of it, but you do not
know where it comes from or where it goes.
So it is with everyone who is born of the Spirit.'

John 3:8

Prayers of Thanksgiving and Intercession

For your Spirit woven into the fabric of creation
for the eternal overlapping with time
and the life of earth interlaced with heaven's vitality
I give you thanks, O God.
For your untamed creativity
your boundless mystery
and your passionate yearnings
planted deep in the soul of every human being
I give you thanks.
Grant me the grace to reclaim these depths
to uncover this treasure
to liberate these longings
and in being set free in my own spirit
to act for the well-being of the world.

*Recall the events of the day
and pray for the life of the world*

Closing Prayer

O Brother Jesus
who wept at the death of a friend
and overturned tables in anger at wrong
let me not be frightened by the depths of passion.
Rather let me learn the love and anger
and wild expanses of soul within me
that are true expressions of your grace and wisdom.
And assure me again that in becoming more like you
I come closer to my true self
made in the image of outpouring Love
born of the free eternal Wind.

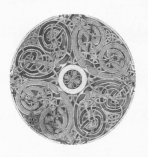

MONDAY NIGHT PRAYER

Tuesday
Morning
Prayer

'I lift up my eyes to the hills –
from where will my help come?
My help comes from God,
who made heaven and earth.'

Psalm 121:1-2

SILENCE

*Be still and aware of God's presence within
and all around*

Opening Prayer

In the beginning, O God,
when the firm earth emerged from the waters of life
you saw that it was good.
The fertile ground was moist
the seed was strong
and earth's profusion of colour and scent was born.
Awaken my senses this day
to the goodness that still stems from Eden.
Awaken my senses
to the goodness that can still spring forth
in me and in all that has life.

Scripture and Meditation

'O taste and see that God is good.'

Psalm 34:2

'I came that you may have life, and
have it abundantly.'   *John 10:10*

Prayers of Thanksgiving and Intercession

The world is alive with your goodness, O God,
it grows green from the ground
and ripens into the roundness of fruit.
Its taste and its touch
enliven my body and stir my soul.
Generously given
profusely displayed
your graces of goodness pour forth from the earth.
As I have received
so free me to give.
As I have been granted
so may I give.

Pray for the coming day
and for the life of the world

Closing Prayer

I have tasted the fruit of the earth, O God.
I have seen autumn trees hang heavily with heaven's gifts.
I have known people pregnant with your spirit of generosity.
Let these be guides to me this day.
And may Mary who knew her womb filled with
your goodness
teach me the wisdom that is born amidst pain.
May I know that deeper than any fallowness in me
is the seed planted in the womb of my soul.
May I know that greater than any barrenness in the world
is the harvest to be justly shared.

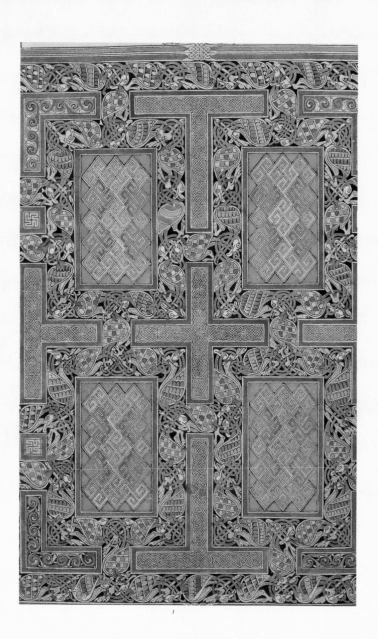

Tuesday
Night
Prayer

'For you alone, O God, my soul waits in silence,
from you comes my salvation.' *Psalm 62:1*

SILENCE

*Be still and aware of God's presence within
and all around*

Opening Prayer

O God of the high mountains
O Christ of the fertile valleys
O Spirit of the earth
from whose dark soils burst forth fresh life
and from which my own body and soul are born
be to me this night
the bestower of grace.
Be to my body and soul this night
the generous giver of love.

Scripture and Meditation

'The earth is full of your goodness, O God.'

Psalm 33:5

'Unless a grain of wheat falls into the earth
and dies, it remains just a single grain;
but if it dies, it bears much fruit.' *John 12:24*

Prayers of Thanksgiving and Intercession

For earth's cycles and seasons
for the rising of spring and the growing summer
for autumn's fullness and the hidden depths of winter
thanks be to you, O Christ.
For the life force in seeds buried in the ground
that shoot green and bear fruit and fall to the earth
thanks be to you.
Let me learn from earth's cycles of birthing
the times and seasons of dying.
Let me learn of you in the soil of my soul, O Christ,
and your journey through death to birth.
Let me learn of you in my soul this night
and the journey of letting go.

*Recall the events of the day
and pray for the life of the world*

Closing Prayer

Glory be to you O Holy Seed of all that has been born
for earth, sea and sky in vibrancy of colour.
Glory be to you O Light of Life
for your liberation of earth's bound treasures.
Glory be to you O River of delight
surging through the heart of creation.
Renew me this night in the depths of sleep,
set free my dreams of the unknown.
Safeguard this time of resting, O God,
enfold me in the darkness of the night.

Wednesday Morning Prayer

'Awake, my soul!
I will awake the dawn,
and give you thanks, O God.'

Psalm 57:8-9

SILENCE

*Be still and aware of God's presence within
and all around*

Opening Prayer

With the rising of the sun
life rises again within me, O God.
In the dawning of the morning light
you lead me from the mists of the night
into the clarity of the day.
In the new light of this day
bring me to a clearer knowing
of the mystery that first bore me from the dark.
Bring me to a clearer knowing
of the love from which all life is born.

Scripture and Meditation

'Let me hear of your steadfast love in the morning
for in you I put my trust.'   *Psalm 143:8*

Jesus said, 'This is my commandment,
that you love one another as I have loved you.'
                                                John 15:12

Prayers of Thanksgiving and Intercession

For the first showings of the morning light
and the emerging outline of the day
thanks be to you, O God.
For earth's colours drawn forth by the sun
its brilliance piercing clouds of darkness
and shimmering through leaves and flowing waters
thanks be to you.
Show to me this day
amidst life's dark streaks of wrong and suffering
the light that endures in every person.
Dispel the confusions that cling close to my soul
that I may see with eyes washed by your grace
that I may see myself and all people
with eyes cleansed by the freshness of the new day's light.

Pray for the coming day
and for the life of the world

Closing Prayer

O Sun behind all suns
O Soul within all souls
grant me the grace of the dawn's glory
grant me the strength of the sun's rays
that I may be well in my own soul
and part of the world's healing this day
that I may be well in my own soul
and part of the world's healing this day.

Wednesday Night Prayer

'Yours is the day, yours also the night;
you made the luminaries of the sky,
the sun, moon and stars.' *Psalm 74:16*

SILENCE

*Be still and aware of God's presence within
and all around*

Opening Prayer

Glory be to you, O God of the night,
for the whiteness of the moon
and the infinite stretches of dark space.
Let me be learning to love the night
as I know and love the day.
Let me be learning to trust its darkness
and to seek its subtle blessings.
Let me be learning the night's way of seeing
that in all things I may trace the mystery
of your presence.

Scripture and Meditation

'Lead me in your truth and teach me
for you are the God of my salvation.'

Psalm 25:5

Jesus said, 'You will know the truth,
and the truth will set you free.'

John 8:32

Prayers of Thanksgiving and Intercession

That you have placed a harmony of lights in the heavens
that night is followed by day
and the glowing of the moon by the glistening of the sun
thanks be to you, O God.
That you have placed a harmony of lights in my soul
that there is gentleness and firmness of strength
intuitive knowing and enlightened reasoning
thanks be to you.
Let me be so sure of your law of harmony in all things
that I seek it in my own depths
and in knowing it in my inner life
yearn for it in the torn relationships of my world
man and woman
black and white
sun and moon in a harmony of movement.

Recall the events of the day
and pray for the life of the world

Closing Prayer

In the beginning, O God,
you placed seeds in the womb of the earth.
On the surface of the earth and in its seas and skies
you made male and female of every species.
And above the earth
you called the two great lights into relationship.
Renew me this night
in the fruitful intermingling that you have woven into creation
that I may wake to the morning
enlivened by love
that I may wake to the morning
enlivened by love.

Thursday Morning Prayer

'You show me the path of life, O God.
In your presence there is fullness of joy.'

Psalm 16:11

SILENCE

*Be still and aware of God's presence within
and all around*

Opening Prayer

As the light of dawn awakens earth's creatures
and stirs into song the birds of the morning
so may I be brought to life this day.
Rising to see the light
to hear the wind
to smell the fragrance of what grows from the ground
to taste its fruit
and touch its textures
so may my inner senses be awakened to you
so may my senses be awakened to you, O God.

Scripture and Meditation

'You satisfy the thirsty,
and fill the hungry with good things.'

Psalm 107:9

Jesus said, 'I am the bread of life'.

John 6:35

Prayers of Thanksgiving and Intercession

That you formed my body in the darkness of the womb
and fashioned every creature from the soil of the earth
thanks be to you, O God.
That you knitted into my senses
a thirst for water and a hunger for food
and wove into every living being
desires for life
and pleasure in their satisfaction
thanks be to you.
Let me be alert
to the yearnings that you have placed within me
and let me know what will truly satisfy the desires of my heart.
Let me be attentive
to the yearnings that you have planted in every human being
and let me be sure of what will fulfil them.
Let me be guided by your wisdom, O Christ,
let me be guided by your wisdom.

Pray for the coming day
and for the life of the world

Closing Prayer

The vitality of God be mine this day
the vitality of the God of life.
The passion of Christ be mine this day
the passion of the Christ of love.
The wakefulness of the Spirit be mine this day
the wakefulness of the Spirit of justice.
The vitality and passion and wakefulness of God be mine
that I may be fully alive this day
the vitality and passion and wakefulness of God
that I may be fully alive.

Thursday Night Prayer

'As a deer longs for flowing streams,
so my soul longs for you, O God.
My soul thirsts for God,
for the living God.'   *Psalm 42:1-2*

SILENCE

*Be still and aware of God's presence within
and all around*

Opening Prayer

In the darkness of the evening
the eyes of my heart are awake to you.
In the quiet of the night
I long to hear again intimations of your love.
In the sufferings of the world
and the struggles of my life
I seek your graces of healing.
At the heart of the brokenness around me
and in the hidden depths of my own soul
I seek your touch of healing, O God,
for there you reside.
In the hidden depths of life, O God,
there you reside.

Scripture and Meditation

'You turn a desert into pools of water,
a parched land into springs of water.'

Psalm 107:35

Jesus said, 'I am the resurrection and the life.'

John 11:25

Prayers of Thanksgiving and Intercession

When it seemed there was no hope
I have seen your light in the eyes of a child.
When it seemed there was no joy
I have heard your delight in the voice of a friend.
When it seemed that life was stale
I have smelled the freshness of sunlight on my skin.
When all seemed emptiness
I have touched your presence in the hand of a stranger.
When the future seemed barren
I have tasted life's moisture on the lips of another.
Thanks be to you, O God,
for your embodied love.
Open my senses to your presence
that I may love you and care for you in all things.

Recall the events of the day
and pray for the life of the world

Closing Prayer

You have given me eyes to see with, O God,
and ears to hear life's sounds and sorrows
and yet my seeing and hearing
like my tasting and touching
are wounded and weakened by failures.
As rest can heal the sores of a body
and sleep restores its strength
so may your angels of grace visit me in the night
that the senses of my soul may be born afresh.
Visit my dreams with messengers of grace, O God,
that the senses of my soul may be born again.

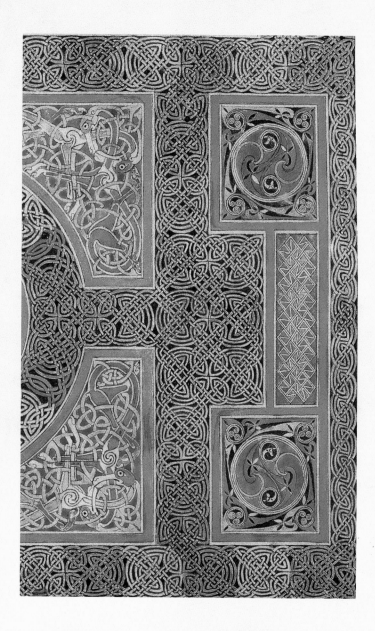

Friday Morning Prayer

'It was you, O God, who made my inmost self,
you knit me together in my mother's womb.
I praise you, for I am fearfully and wonderfully made.'

Psalm 139:13-14

SILENCE

*Be still and aware of God's presence within
and all around*

Opening Prayer

In the morning light, O God,
may I glimpse again your image deep within me
the threads of eternal glory
woven into the fabric of every man and woman.
Again may I catch sight of the mystery of the human soul
fashioned in your likeness
deeper than knowing
more enduring than time.
And in glimpsing these threads of light
amidst the weakness and distortions of my life
let me be recalled
to the strength and beauty deep in my soul.
Let me be recalled
to the strength and beauty of your image in every living soul.

Scripture and Meditation

'You desire truth in the inward being;
therefore teach me wisdom in my secret heart.'

Psalm 51:6

Jesus said, 'The Spirit will guide you into all truth.'

John 16:13

Prayers of Thanksgiving and Intercession

That wisdom was born with me in the womb
thanks be to you, O God.
That your ways have been written into
the human body and soul
there to be read and reverenced
thanks be to you.
Let me be attentive
to the truths of these living texts.
Let me learn
of the law etched into the whole of creation
that gave birth to the mystery of life
and feeds and renews it day by day.
Let me discern the law of love in my own heart
and in knowing it
obey it.
Let me be set free by love, O God.
Let me be set free to love.

Pray for the coming day
and for the life of the world

Closing Prayer

Glory be to you, O God,
for the gift of life
unfolding through those who have gone before me.
Glory be to you, O God,
for your life planted within my soul
and in every soul coming into the world.
Glory be to you, O God,
for the grace of new beginnings
placed before me in every moment and encounter of life.
Glory, glory, glory
for the grace of new beginnings in every moment of life.

Friday Night Prayer

'When I look at the heavens, the work of your hands,
the moon and the stars that you have made;
what are human beings that you are mindful of them,
children of the earth that you care for them?
Yet you have created us a little lower than the angels,
and crowned us with glory and honour.'   *Psalm 8:3-5*

SILENCE

*Be still and aware of God's presence within
and all around*

Opening Prayer

For the night skies opening outwards
star upon star
expanse after expanse
thanks be to you, O God.
For the mystery of your presence
in and beyond all that can be seen
thanks be to you.
Guide me further this night
into the inner universe of my soul
ever opening inwards
light upon light
new depth after new depth.
Guide me through strange and fearful spaces
towards the place of your eternal dwelling
and assure me again that in drawing closer to you
I draw closer to the heart of every living being
that in drawing closer to you
I approach the heart of life.

Scripture and Meditation

'I delight to do your will, O my God;
your law is within my heart.'

Psalm 40:8

Jesus said, 'It is the spirit that gives life.'

John 6:63

Prayers of Thanksgiving and Intercession

That life is conceived out of passion
and that your passion for life
has been sown within every human being
thanks be to you, O God.
For the desires in women and men for children
and the life-long yearnings of mothers and fathers
for the well-being of their sons and daughters
thanks be to you.
For the hopes of friends for one another
and the cries of whole societies and nations
for justice and freedom for their people
thanks be to you.
Rekindle in me your passion for life, O God,
rekindle in me your passion for life.

*Recall the events of the day
and pray for the life of the world*

CELTIC BENEDICTION

ST. MARY'S HIGH SCHOOL

Closing Prayer

Renew me this night in the image of your love
renew me in the likeness of your mercy, O God.
May any refusal to forgive
that lingers with me from the day
any bitterness of soul
that hardens my heart
be softened by your graces of the night.
Renew me in the image of your love, O God,
renew me in the likeness of your mercy.

Saturday Morning Prayer

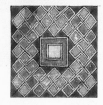

'Long ago you laid the foundations of the earth
and the heavens are the work of your hands.
They will perish but you endure;
they wear out like garments
but you are the same and your years have no end.'

Psalm 102:25-27

SILENCE

*Be still and aware of God's presence within
and all around*

Opening Prayer

In the silence of the early morning
your Spirit hovers over the brink of the day
and new light pierces the darkness of the night.
In the silence of the morning
life begins to stir around me
and I listen for the day's first utterances.
In earth, sea and sky
and in the landscape of my own soul
I listen for utterances of your love, O God.
I listen for utterances of your love.

Scripture and Meditation

'Be still and know that I am God.'

Psalm 46:10

Jesus said, 'I give you eternal life,
and you will never perish.'

John 10:28

Prayers of Thanksgiving and Intercession

For the night followed by the day
for the idle winter ground
followed by the energy of spring
for the infolding of the earth
followed by bursts of unfolding
thanks be to you, O God.
For rest and wakefulness
stillness and creativity
reflection and action
thanks be to you.
Let me know in my own soul and body
the rhythms of creativity that you have established.
Let me know in my family and friendships
the disciplines of withdrawal and the call to engagement.
Let me know for my world
the cycles of renewal
given by you for healing and health
the pattern of the seasons
given by you for the birth of new life.

Pray for the coming day
and for the life of the world

CELTIC BENEDICTION

Closing Prayer

In the busyness of this day
grant me a stillness of seeing, O God.
In the conflicting voices of my heart
grant me a calmness of hearing.
Let my seeing and hearing
my words and my actions
be rooted in a silent certainty of your presence.
Let my passions for life
and the longings for justice that stir within me
be grounded in the experience of your stillness.
Let my life be rooted in the ground of your peace, O God,
let me be rooted in the depths of your peace.

Saturday Night Prayer

'Blessed are you, O God, for you give me counsel;
in the night also my heart instructs me.'

Psalm 16:7

SILENCE

*Be still and aware of God's presence within
and all around*

Opening Prayer

As it was in the stillness of the morning
so may it be in the silence of the night.
As it was in the hidden vitality of the womb
so may it be at my birth into eternity.
As it was in the beginning, O God,
so in the end may your gift be born
so in the end may your gift of life be born.

Scripture and Meditation

'With my whole heart I seek you, O God,
I treasure your word in my heart.'

Psalm 119:10-11

Jesus said, 'Peace I leave with you;
my peace I give to you.
Do not let your hearts be troubled,
and do not let them be afraid.'

John 14:27

Prayers of Thanksgiving and Intercession

For the darkness of the night
enveloping the earth
enclosing the day's labour
thanks be to you, O God.
For the quiet that surrounds me
and your promise of peace deep within me
for the stillness of sleep for my body
and the hope of healing for my soul
thanks be to you.
I bring not only my own weariness
but the tiredness of people who struggle this night.
I bring not only my own pain
but the sufferings of those who cry out.
Hear my soul's prayers for rest, O God,
hear my heart's plea for healing.

Recall the events of the day
and pray for the life of the world

Closing Prayer

The stillness of God be mine this night
that I may sleep in peace.
The awareness of the angels be mine this night
that I may be alert to unseen mysteries.
The company of the saints be mine this night
that I may dream of the river of love.
The life of Christ be mine this night
that I may be truly alive to the morning
that I may be truly alive.

APPENDIX

Celtic Art Illustrations

The art illustrations used throughout this book are taken from the Lindisfarne Gospels, a thirteen-hundred-year-old collection of gospel manuscripts from the holy island of Lindisfarne off the Northumbrian coast in north-east England. They are now housed in the British Museum Library in London.

The monastic community of Lindisfarne was part of the ancient Celtic mission of Ireland that stretched through Scotland into England by the 7th century. St Aidan of Iona established the community in the year 635 on the little tidal island off the Northumbrian coastline near Berwick-upon-Tweed. Twice a day at high tide the sea engulfs Lindisfarne cutting it off from the mainland. At low tide miles of white beach surround the island and make it accessible by a natural causeway of sand stretching across the sea. Here the monastic community thrived and its mission expanded. By the end of the century it had produced the beautiful illuminated manuscripts of the Lindisfarne Gospels.

All of the artwork and calligraphy is attributed to one monk, Eadfrith, who later became Bishop of Lindisfarne in 698. The detailed work of copying and decorating the gospel texts took years of continuous work. The calfskin vellum on which he wrote and painted was of local origin but Eadfrith's sources for the brilliant colours used throughout his work were from all over the then-known world. They included indigo from the Orient and blue lapis lazuli from the Himalayas.

Eadfrith's imaginative eye and skill of execution are extraordinary but the themes that dominate the illuminated gospel texts of Lindisfarne are typical of the great works of Celtic art that come to fullest expression in this and the next number of centuries. The combination of creation motifs with a devotion to Christ is what distinguishes this tradition from the religious art of the Mediterranean mission. Flowing patterns of what are like interweaving vines, in which creatures of earth, sea and sky are interlaced, speak of the inter-relatednesss of all things. Spirals of life and circles of wholeness integrate imagery from creation into an explicitly religious work of art and contemplation.

Eadfrith's most sophisticated and intricate artwork is achieved in what are known as 'carpet' pages and major 'initial' pages that precede the four gospel texts of Matthew, Mark, Luke and John. In the Lindisfarne Gospels the former are known as 'cross-carpet' pages because they are centred on images of the cross. Eadfrith also includes diamond shapes to represent the person of Christ. This is typical of the Celtic tradition. Its celebration of creation is linked inseparably with its Christ mysticism. As St Paul says, 'In Christ all things hold together' (Colossians 1:17). Likewise, Celtic artists repeatedly choose to weave together themes of creation with themes of redemption. Both are regarded as flowing forth from the mystery of God. The gift of grace is given not in opposition to the gift of nature but to restore to life again the goodness planted by God at the heart of nature.

It is this combination in the artwork of the Lindisfarne Gospels that is forever inviting us to look for layers of meaning, not only in the illuminated pages of gospel text but in ourselves and in the whole of creation. Its imagery and forms are not realistic representations of outward daily life. Rather they are suggestive and almost dreamlike visions of the eternal. The invitation is to look with wonder at life, not only with our physical sight but, as the Celtic tradition says, with 'the eyes of the heart'.